SNAKES & ADDERS

A SET UP FOR THE STEP UP

Fiona Onasanya

‌ʰop Dr. Wayne Malcolm

Bible references are from the King James Version

Cover design & layout by David Springer 2019
The pencil drawing is by Tony Nero 2019
The photgraph (which was sketched)
is from The Moment Magazine,
the Editor of which is Mark Wilson.

Table of Contents

Acknowledgements

Mummy! Your love knows no bounds. Thank you for always being there, from standing with me to praying for me. I thank God for your life.

My bestie, Kimbo – you have no idea how your listening ear and shoulder to lean on have carried me through. You have gone above and beyond the call of duty and I'm overwhelmed that you would call me friend.

A very special thanks to Uncle Mordi and Papa B for your enduring encouragement, all those individuals with whom I have been privileged to cross paths with on this journey called life, my helpers who have supported me and lastly, the haters!

Dedication/Declaration

*Having reviewed other
books I noticed it is usual to write
a dedication, but rather than be usual,
I believe it necessary to decree and
declare in accordance with Job 22 v 28!
Without God, I could not stand. He is
the author and finisher of my faith and
with Him, this has all been possible.*

Foreword

It was surreal. Sitting in the public gallery at the Old Bailey in a courtroom where cases of murder and terrorism are typically tried. Opposite a huge press presence taking vigorous notes. Sitting next to me was the mother of Fiona Onasanya and the fiancée of Festus Onasanya, together with a small group of close friends.

I've known her mother, "Lady P" for 30 years or more. Although our local ministry was London based and she was primarily based in Cambridge, we were all part of the same church denomination which convened numerous conventions and church anniversary celebrations throughout the year. This meant that we were always together in some service, somewhere, up and down the country. Additionally Lady P never passed up an opportunity to attend our local church conferences and special events. So it was as though we were all in the same church and meeting on a weekly basis. Fiona was the little girl in church with her mum who was known as the fiery Evangelist from Cambridge.

The years went by and little Fiona emerged as a young aspirational woman. It was then that she became a fully fledged member of our local church, despite residing some distance away. Every Sunday, there she was; the aspirational role model Fiona. Unlike many of her peers in our young adults ministry, she seemed to possess an uncommon sense of focus and personal discipline. Once she set her sights on a goal, she wouldn't be swayed or distracted by the usual suspects. Parties, boys, drinking and the like were not her thing. Instead it was education, qualifications and professional progress. Don't get me wrong; she was normal in every way but chose to pay the price today for a better tomorrow. She made lots of conscious sacrifices to achieve her academic and professional goal of an exciting career in law.

Although it wasn't obvious to some that she would eventually go into politics, I secretly harboured that hunch. This was because of my frequently overhearing her defending the rights of citizens. Matters of social justice or the lack thereof and economic disparity would really annoy her. She would argue with passion for a better system, a fairer system, a level playing field and a just society. In hindsight there was obviously a little politician in there. It soon became undeniable that Fiona had a role to play in politics and as her Pastor, I prayed with her and encouraged her to go with her unique flow.

I remember when she became a Cambridgeshire Councillor and how seriously she took the role. It came as no surprise that she quickly ascended the ranks to become a major force in the County Council and a rising star in the Labour Party. The events that lead to her subsequent election as Labour MP for Peterborough North, are nothing short of epic. None of us slept that night, waiting in anticipation for the results. The joy we all felt when we realised that she had won. Little Fi had won in what had been a Tory seat for over 12 years to the shock of everyone including her own party members who didn't think she could do it.

I guess I could go on about Fiona's rise, but back to the court! I'm in the courtroom at the Old Bailey listening to a Judge sentencing her to prison. I couldn't pinch myself hard enough. I needed to wake up. This couldn't be happening. What has she done? Why is this happening? How is this happening? This can't be about a speeding ticket - can it? In the following days I listened, read and watched press outlets, pundits and commentators demonising an amazing lady; literally trashing her character and rubbishing her achievements. I read venomous posts on social media equating her with the devil and wishing her even more harm. Some of the comments were clearly politically motivated and others were outright racist.

This sense of disbelief was compounded when I found out that she would serve out her sentence in a prison alongside category A prisoners convicted for murder, terrorism and child molestation. All this for allegedly giving false information about who was driving her car when it was captured by camera breaking the speed limit; or so the public thought! It turns out in the end that she was found guilty, not of providing false information but of apparently knowing that her brother provided false information and not reporting it! She had a clean licence and three points wouldn't have impacted her career. He had 9 points on his licence and three more points would have ended his job as a driver. He openly admitted to filling out the form because he thought he was driving the car and needed to cover himself just in case.

It was pretty obvious to me what had happened and in my humble opinion, the Judge, at sentencing, was also clear about who filled out the form and why, but faced with 'public pressure' had to sentence someone with no previous convictions and no motive for the crime to 3 months in prison.

Whatever my beliefs about the truth in this matter or my suspicions about the motivations behind the prosecution, verdict and sentencing, I emerged from the whole experience with a very simple conclusion: Our political system (including its component parts) is fundamentally broken and without serious repair will continue to fail us all.

I don't think this is the end for Fiona and am praying that one day, her truth will be known. There are some facts of life that you simply cannot learn through academic education alone. You can only know them by experience. Fiona now knows by experience what others speculate about through reading. I hope that her story will help to start a meaningful conversation about politics, law and criminal justice in the UK. With that, I commend this book to you.

Bishop Wayne Malcolm

Preface

I'd always said I wanted to write a book called "The Journey" and now given recent events I think it's quite apt!

It got me thinking, the Bible is absolutely right in Psalms 37 v 23 when it says "The steps of a good man are ordered by the Lord...." For me this has become so apparent now!

Most people would question why I choose to remain strong in my faith, but I honestly don't know how people go through this journey called life without Him.

Introduction

Considering 'steps', I remember the board game Snakes and Ladders and thinking it is quite symbolic. This journey called life is full of peaks and troughs, but this was something very different.

No-one tells you that at the top of ladders can be a pit of adders!!!

Adders are Britain's only venomous snake but in the world of politics, I think there are two types which come disguised as what I will call constituents and comrades!!

I do not refer to constituents and comrades in the true meaning of the words, I am referring to constituents as those people who share your ideals and support your vision but do not necessarily support you.

Comrades fight the same battles, they are against the same things you are and fight with you for a common purpose but they are not for you! Neither group should be considered confidants anymore than Adders should be considered ladders!

Armed with this knowledge – the title of this book became clear as the beginning of my story.

CHAPTER 01

A GAME?

*I have always said that life
is a journey, not a destination –
but is it a game?!*

It's surreal to think that a conversation in a pub had culminated in my selection and subsequent positioning in Parliament.

I can't recall the friend I met with, but I remember the name of the pub, The Burleigh Arms and the fact we were discussing the London riots.

I remember that the reason given for the riots, began with individuals claiming this response was a public outcry – *but did criminal damage and violence really address the issue?*

I had asked my friend if they truly believed the Prime Minister was unaware of information plastered all over social media?! When, driving through central London without paying the congestion charge, could be picked up by midnight of the day in which it was incurred - *how were Government unaware?*

My personal view was that neither the Prime Minister or Government cared.

Why would they?!

Did the smashing up and looting of shops directly affect them? I didn't think so! *This was not an outcry for justice.* It was then that the gentleman interjected; "I hope you don't mind but I eavesdropped on your conversation, have you ever thought about going into politics?"

I looked at him rather quizzically, 'NO! Law is my thing' – "Politics is, like Shakespeare once said; 'Much Ado About Nothing'." A wry smile spread across his face, "Why don't you look into what we do, I think you'd be really good at it!" Now I must admit, I felt this was a challenge, *I'll show him!* "Who's we?!" I replied.

He explained his name was Nader Khalifa and he was the Secretary for the Cambridge Labour Party. Well that was like a red rag to a bull! **"Labour"** I retorted, "Labour?! After the war in Iraq?!" But Nader was not perturbed. It seemed that my behaviour and tone had not caused him to think twice about his approach, rather he informed me that the Party was under new leadership and invited me to go online to look at their manifesto - an offer which I respectfully accepted.

Just like a game, I intended to have the upper hand. My thoughts were that I would look into what Labour stood for, review their manifesto and report back setting out all the errors and reasons I had come across as to why Labour was not the right choice and where they had gone wrong!

This was the start.

In a game you sometimes know the players – but you have no idea how it will end, who will win and how those who don't will handle defeat!

The only fact known, agreed and understood by all is that we are playing!

Winning is a hope or aspiration in the minds of the players – but to begin with it's fun being in the game.

This is why I always say you do not win or lose, you win or learn!

CHAPTER 02

LET'S PLAY!

I can't remember now whether I got home that evening and googled Labour or whether it was the next day, I only remember how intrigued I felt when I left the pub that evening.

I remember poring over the manifesto and realising Labour was a movement for all and a movement for good. They sought to empower people, to give those struggling a hand up, not a hand out. As I continued to read with interest, I began to realise that whilst I did not agree with everything, there were at least 7 out of 10 key principles that I did agree with.

The principal fundamental factor that attracted me was social justice.

After I concluded my research, I found myself reaching for my debit card and paying a small fee (£3 I think!) to become a member of the Labour Party.

Looking back, I do smile to think my intention was to conduct research, in order to discredit the Party and further bolster my disparaging remarks. Yet here I was, a new member having found this movement aligned almost perfectly with my desire for change and a belief in better.

CHAPTER 03

MY TURN?

H ere I was, turning 28 years old – not a clue about politics – yet a member of a political party?!

At the pub Nader had given me his business card, so I contacted him to let him know I'd become a member. He then let me have the time, address and date of the next "GC meeting." Now one thing politics is full of are acronyms!! So I was like, "What's a GC?!"

Coming from a legal background I've had my fair share of acronyms – even my legal studies were baptised with them; an LLB (Hons) degree in Law and my postgraduate LPC (Legal Practice Course). These had shown me that many professions or sectors embrace the use of acronyms, but I wasn't afraid to ask what they meant! You don't know what you don't know!!

Nader not only explained that this was a General Committee meeting, but also went on to advise that all party members could attend and I could learn a lot about the issues that mattered most, the impact Labour was having locally and what future plans or proposals were.

This resonated with me because I am a great believer that failing to plan is planning to fail! So I advised I would certainly like to attend.

The evening of the GC came around really quickly. I got my bike and cycled to Alex Wood Hall. There were a few people already there when I arrived. "Would you like a tea or coffee?", "No thank you", I replied; "I don't drink tea or coffee!" The person asking looked quite surprised. Recalling it now makes me wonder if they believed me or thought that was my way of declining an offer of a hot drink. That said, I was more than happy to help myself to a biccy (or two!).

"Can you all take your seats, we are about to start" a voice bellowed out. I was more than happy to oblige and took my seat, the room had filled up by this point and I looked around smiling enthusiastically.

The meeting began and I remember feeling quite bamboozled - people talking over one another – a chap stood saying he had a motion, he was asked to sit back down and wait until after we had concluded matters arising – then there was a need to verify that the previous minutes were an accurate record – all whilst there were mumbles and the sound of pages turning.

I don't recall how or when we got into the detail of the meeting, but I do remember suddenly raising my hand to ask what LCF meant. "It's the Local Campaign Forum" someone answered. After several interjections from me with a raised hand I learnt that the LA was the Local Authority, SEN were Special Educational Needs and what sounded like neat was in fact NEET – Not in Employment Education or Training.

To listen to it was so interesting and intriguing – I remember feeling that there was so much to learn and I was eager to do so.

CHAPTER 04

THE FIRST MOVE?

Members were advised there were 'wards' that required canvassing and leafletting. *Wards? Canvassing? What were these?!* I was told I could "Buddy up" with someone to learn the ropes if I was interested - *interested?! Of course I was!* So I added my name, email address and number to the list that was being circulated. I explained to the person beside the table that I lived in Chesterton and was free over the weekend so I was more than happy to help out in the area *or ward as they called it* and with that, I left, unlocked my bike and cycled home.

I think it was the following Saturday when I first went door knocking and leafleting with the East Chesterton team of people.

Now, I'm not a shy person by any stretch of the imagination so the idea of getting to talk to people and help find solutions for them was great! I watched the first pair knock but no one was there so a leaflet was placed in their letterbox. I recall being advised that one had to be careful not to put your fingers in/through the letterbox as pets may think they were treats!

After a few more 'outs' someone opened their door.
I listened intently as the person who knocked explained who we were and why we were there.

The person answering the door shared how parking was an issue and the canvasser took notes – *I can do this* I thought. I then offered to knock doors and did so, collating information and speaking to residents.

At the end of the afternoon we had spoken to quite a few people and collated lots of data. I'd quite enjoyed it and as I'm very much a solution-oriented person I was only too happy to work with others to find a way forwards – after all, a problem shared is a problem solved because a problem is only an opportunity in disguise!

It was only a short time after this, that Nader got in touch again.

By this time, although I'd been to a few more GC meetings, observed an EC (Executive Committee) meeting, delivered leaflets and even been canvassing without a buddy!

For Nader to say "I thought of you" when a local election was coming up was somewhat surprising. *Did Nader realise what he was saying? He seriously wanted me to apply to be a Cambridge City Councillor candidate?! Waaaaow!!!*

"You probably won't win the selection, but it'll be good experience..." I never stopped to think, *good experience for what?* And to be fair I never asked, but it sounded like a challenge I was up for.

"Okay" I interjected as Nader was explaining what the selection process would entail, "I'll give it a bash." "Great" he replied. "So what does a Councillor do then?!" I asked. Nader laughed "Exactly what you're doing now! Helping others – a type of advocate for the people."

'Umm' I thought to myself, *that's a fair point,* "Yeah okay, I'm in" I said.

CHAPTER 05

WHERE NEXT?

Now I'd agreed to be a potential candidate for the City Councillor selections, I felt I had to do my research, so I went to the library. Looking at the City Council website and enquiring of others what the Council did and what the role was like. It was very interesting to read about services the City Council provided (as Cambridge also had a County Council), how many Councillors sat on the Council, review past papers and learn about which Councillors served which areas of the City. Armed with this knowledge and information I turned my attention to the notes I had taken about what Nader had called "The Selection Process."

I had never prepared a speech before, *I know I talk lots (and gesticulate loads!) But how should a Councillor sound? Should speeches be read? Or rehearsed so they are memorised?* These were just some of the questions I had contemplated, I was nervously expectant – *Just be yourself* were the words that continued to resound in my head – *but what did that even mean?!*

With that thought I gathered my belongings together and got up to leave thinking about how I should start my speech.

Some days and weeks had passed - I'd cobbled some stuff together and announced over dinner one Sunday "Mum, do you wanna hear my speech?" "Hold on let me just grab something from the kitchen" came the reply.

I sat reading and re-reading my speech whilst mum nipped into the kitchen. Min. David had come back to ours after Church and sat smiling at the prospect of what he was about to hear.

Mum returned from the kitchen to join Bea, Min. David and I, "Go on then" mum said. I took a breath, sat up in my seat and began:

"My name is Fiona Onasanya and I am from East Chesterton. I stand here before you today to ask for your support to become the City Councillor for this ward, in which I live...." The speech lasted for a little under 5 minutes (I had timed myself as 5 minutes was the maximum time allowed). When I'd finished I sat back and placed the paper down on the table. There was a moments silence, then an applause from the three of them. I sat smiling.

Min. David offered advice: "Look up when you're speaking, try to only glance down rather than just reading what you've written aloud and smile," I nodded – this made so much sense I just had to work out how to put it into practice.

CHAPTER 06

IS IT MY TURN?

Having rehearsed my speech to anyone willing to listen, the day of selection finally arrived. I picked my outfit of a tailored blouse, grey pencil skirt, small heels and stud earrings in addition to my tanned briefcase and hair tied back, I was ready!

This time I drove to Alex Wood Hall, rather than cycling (as I didn't want to arrive a hot dishevelled mess!), parked opposite the Hall and sat in the car for a moment.

This felt just like an interview! *C'mon Fiona, you've got this* I said to myself as I got out of the car.

I retrieved my briefcase from the car, straightened out my skirt and changed into my heels, *I wonder what the panel will be like?*

I crossed the road and approached the door. "Here goes" I muttered to myself as I rang the door buzzer to gain access.

There was no answer but the entry buzzer was pressed so I could open the door, I breathed in, pushed on the door handle and entered.

I remember walking into the Hall where we'd had so many GC meetings before, the kitchen was opposite the door, there were double doors to the left – closed this time…. *Was I supposed to go in?*

I gingerly entered the hall where five people sat behind tables, I said "Hello" in the chirpiest voice I could muster and they duly replied. I walked over to a chair to place my briefcase down, walked over to a central position in front of them, held my speech and began speaking whilst looking across the panel, and as Min. David had advised, remembering to smile.

The 5 minutes flew by, it was all over – I hadn't stumbled on my words, or read too much, I'd explained who I was and why I thought I'd be the best candidate choice. I'd covered what I believed were the issues in my area (ward) and set out the steps I thought could and should be taken to combat these and make a tangible difference. I was really happy with how it went, I asked if there were any questions for me, then thanked them, went over to the chair, collected my briefcase and left the hall to await the outcome in a side room.

Whilst waiting I heard the other candidate enter the hall – she didn't come into the side room to wait when she'd finished - I don't recall exactly where she was when I was called back in - "Fiona." Hearing my name I scurried to my feet and walked back into the hall. "Hi Fiona, thank you so much for coming today, we can see how much you care about your ward and the residents who live there.

You were an impressive candidate but unfortunately on this occasion we have decided with 3 votes to 2 that the other candidate would be our choice. Please do not give up as we are sure you will go far and maybe next time, be successful." "Thank you for the opportunity and taking the time to listen and consider me" I replied. I shook each of their hands and clutching my briefcase, I left the building and returned to my parked car.

I unlocked my car, and chambered in. I remember thinking I needed to call Nader as I chucked my briefcase on the front passenger seat.

Whilst I sat there I was smiling like a Cheshire cat! *I can't believe they thought I would go far – little old me! This is crazy! What had they seen in me?! I had just made a speech –* I had the paper in my hands though?? *I was just stating the obvious no?!* I called Nader, "Hey Fi, how'd it go?"

I told him I didn't get it, "But you know me – you win or you learn, you don't lose and as you said - it's good experience." "Yes it is" Nader replied, "I didn't think you'd get it as the other potential is friends with the current sitting Councillor and has many many years of experience" – *that's fair enough* I thought. "Ah well, it is what it is" I replied, "Maybe it's too soon, I haven't been a member for that long yet!" Nader laughed, we said our goodbyes and the call ended.

To be honest, I didn't really think any more about it. I told my mum and Bea that I'd been unsuccessful and thereafter carried on assisting the local Party and working as a Plots Sales Executive.

It must have been a couple of months later that Nader told me about the County Council selections "Go on Fiona" he said, "It'll be great experience for you plus it's an All-Womens Shortlist." "Nader!, as if I'll get that, if I didn't get City, how on earth will I get County?! Isn't that higher than a City Councillor in tiers?" I enquired. "Don't worry about all that, give it a try, what is it that you say?, it's better to try and fail, than fail to try?!" *That's cheeky using something I would say against me.* I thought, but he was right, "Okay Nader, I'll go."

Here we go again I thought to myself – I really didn't seriously consider that this was a viable opportunity as I honestly didn't think I'd be selected, so this time I did not prepare a speech, I refreshed the old one!

The day of the selection arrived and I asked mum to drive me to the selection meeting. This time I didn't get suited and booted, I wore skinny jeans, my UGG®boots and a little brown biker style jacket. "Right mum, I'm ready to go" I said, "Are you going like that?!" Mum said sounding surprised, "Yep" I replied in a cheeky tone, "Okay let's go" she replied.

The selection meeting was in the home of an elderly lady – she was lovely, offered us a wide selection and variety of chocolate biscuits (bought just for us as she was diabetic). The house wasn't far from mine so it didn't take too long for us to arrive. "Thanks mum, I shouldn't be too long, I'll call when I'm done so you can collect me", with that I exited the car.

I opened the back gate and read the sign on the back door which said 'Come in' but I still knocked and shouted "Hello" as I entered.

"Hello?" came the reply, "It's Fiona" I said as I poked my head around the living room door – "Oh Fiona!" came the response from the lady, followed by a massive hug which I happily reciprocated.

"Come in love" she said, before another chap reminded her that I needed to wait with the other candidates in the kitchen – "Oh yes, come on you" she said, took me by the hand and led me behind her to the kitchen.

Once in the kitchen I sat at the small table and began speaking with another lady. She had been a Labour member for over 13 years and had hoped that this time she would be successful in her bid to become a Councillor.

She explained she had experience as a Parish Councillor - I explained I had only been a member for about a year and had no experience bar the City Council Selections.

I think it was then that she was called through. I sat reviewing my speech and reminding myself it could only be 5 mins *if I cross bits out it will probably get down to 4 mins.* "Do you have a pen please?" I asked the gent in the kitchen, "Ummm, there must be one somewhere" came the reply. As he was checking himself and the drawers – the lady who had been through to the panel came back into the kitchen. "How'd it go?!" I asked, "Well - I think" she said – but before I could enquire further – I was called through to the panel.

I walked through the door and took a seat in the armchair. Eight faces looked at me as I sat further forward in the chair and began my spiel "For those of you that I haven't met, my name is Fiona Onasanya and I would like to ask for your support in making me your choice for County Councillor candidate. Although I do not live in this ward, we are only separated by Milton Road, as I live in East Chesterton...." I continued to tell them what I considered were the local issues, some questions were asked of me, (I think only a handful of questions were asked) and then I was invited to excuse myself to the kitchen.

I waited back in the kitchen alone as the other lady had been summoned. I don't remember what I thought about but it seemed like only seconds had passed before I was called back through.

As the lady had gone, I assumed they were calling me to advise I was not successful.

Here I was, sitting in the same chair again.

"So Fiona, having discussed this amongst ourselves, we have decided and agreed that we would like for you to be our County Councillor candidate for Kings Hedges."

WHAT???!!! I was absolutely floored! "Wow, gosh, oh my goodness" were the only words I could muster as the look of excitement and bewilderment spread across my face. "You did want to stand didn't you?!" a male voice enquired – "Yeah sorry" I responded, "It's a bit of a shock as I hadn't expected this!" I explained. We exchanged pleasantries and I subsequently left.

Stepping out of the door I'd entered an hour or so before, I then went back out through the gate and called mum – hanging up promptly as she was there!

"I thought I'd hang around as you said you wouldn't be too long" mum said as I opened the car door.

"Mum guess what?" but before she could reply I shrieked: "They selected me?!, they've asked me to be their candidate!!!!" "Praise God" mum replied smiling.

I recall thinking *wow – what did this all mean? What happens now?*

I felt elated. This feeling of wonderment was soon replaced by a calm feeling of cautious optimism and expectation.

CHAPTER 07

NEXT MOVE?

After my selection came campaigning - door knocking, canvassing, speaking to residents, compiling details of issues and taking up matters with the City/County Council where appropriate. I loved helping others and getting stuck into the role of a Councillor before becoming one. It was an eye opener and made me realise that people don't care how much you know until they know how much you care! They want you to stand up for them and speak truth to power.

The fact finding/information gathering was both interesting and informative but it showed just how much needed to be done and taught me lots about true humility - thinking of yourself less, not thinking less of yourself.

After months and weeks the day of the election was finally here. I had decided on a cerise pink dress, I didn't know what was going to happen but I was ready, ready to win or learn!

Upon arrival to the Guildhall I felt expectant and excited! *What happens next? Where do I go?* I found my way into the main hall where the counting was happening.

The room was buzzing with votes being counted, parties trying to get an idea of how it was going by watching the piles of votes gathering in baskets, the radio station presenters and the press.

Wow I thought to myself as I gazed on in wonderment – here I was, little Fifi in the midst of it all!

It seemed like the counting had gone on for a lifetime, when the Returning Officer took the platform, so much so that the voice over the sound system caught me totally off guard!

I recall smiling as the results were read out.

Now I knew that Cambridge City Council was controlled by the Liberal Democrats (Lib Dem) and the person occupying the County Council seat for Kings Hedges was also a Lib Dem. I assumed as he already held the seat, he would retain it. So when his result of, if I recall correctly, 183 votes was read out first – I thought this signalled him retaining the seat! I did not know that the results are read out in alphabetical order!!!

Whilst I waited with baited breath – I was thinking to myself that if he got 183, with an 11% turnout, I could hope for 175 perhaps?!

I heard my name called, then the figure "716." WHAT?! Oh my goodness!! SEVEN HUNDRED AND SIXTEEN VOTES, *I don't believe it, I need to tell my mum, I got 716 votes, wow – oh gosh – I've won!!!!*

I remember what felt like everyone wanting to speak to me; a radio presenter kept asking how I felt? and whether I had expected to win? "I need to tell my mum" was all I could muster through the massive grin. After receiving the same response to every question the presenter laughed and encouraged me to go.

I could not believe this – I could not stop smiling – the canvassing and surveys had paid off, the leaflet rounds and direct mail shots had an impact. I was a County Councillor!!!

I literally skipped out of the hall clutching my paperwork – *gosh we'd done it! Where's my phone – I need to tell mum!* Outside the Guildhall I telephoned mum as I walked to Mill Road – Mum said she was at Kay's "I'm up the road" I exclaimed – "See you in 10!"

I arrived beaming shortly thereafter, "I can't believe I've won" I exclaimed. Congratulatory text messages were coming through as mum and I hugged.

That feeling of excitement and amazement coupled with a cautious optimism lasted for a while. So much so that when I woke up the following day I felt I almost had to pinch myself when I remembered the events of the previous day – I still couldn't believe that I had been elected as the County Councillor for Kings Hedges! I got up, showered, dressed and ready for work. I cycled in to the office as I did every day but today felt different – I think that day I sat higher, cycled faster and arrived quicker!

Upon arrival to the office I parked my bike, locked up and hurried inside. "Congratulations!" The security chap called out – holding up the paper which had my photographed beaming smile inside –"Thank you so much!" I exclaimed as I walked past.

My office was situated on the first floor and as I took the stairs around to my side of the office I grinned. There on the door was a pink 'CONGRATULATIONS' banner. My desk had been decorated in a similar fashion *awww, this is such a lovely gesture.* Thanking everyone for the banner, cards and congratulatory messages, I settled into work.

After work I spoke with a partner of the firm, setting out the dates I had sent to HR (for my civic leave) and advised that whilst I didn't know what was expected – I was excited! I was now a County Councillor, and remained so for 4 years. In my first year I was the Spokesperson for Children, Young People and Families. In years two and three I became the group Whip, then finally progressed, with unanimous support from the Labour group, in the fourth and final year, to Deputy Leader!

During these four years, I was still working within the field of law, became qualified as a Solicitor and stepped onto the property ladder!

I was thoroughly enjoying life as a Councillor as I was able to assist others and my dream/goal of becoming a Solicitor had been realised however, whilst I found it very fulfilling – it was like having 2 full time jobs!!

I think it was in 2016, the penultimate year of my tenure as County Councillor, but two years after buying my home, that I decided I would not stand for re-election. It had been a wonderful experience but I did not feel I could do both and give my best equally. It was then that I thought I would focus on my legal career and come back to politics – maybe, possibly, in the future, perhaps!

CHAPTER 08

ROLL THE DICE!

I decided that if I was not going to remain a Councillor – I could look for work closer to home! *If I'm focussing on law – perhaps I could get a job at a firm in Peterborough? No more A14 commute! Early starts, late nights and home before dark - Yay!!*

I had thought about this for a while since buying my home in 2014, the commute and my lifestyle were speaking volumes – I could no longer serve two masters – I felt that it was law or politics, but I couldn't do both. I couldn't give both roles and areas of interest 100%, so in making a choice, I kept telling myself delay was not denial, perhaps in the future I'd get back into Politics?

I mean if the next general election is May 2020.... maybe I could try – for the experience – to see what a Prospective Parliamentary Candidate (PPC) had to do?! Yes, that's what I'll do, 'I'll bow out for now and focus on Law. Decision made!

I was still a County Councillor as my 4 year tenure had not yet come to an end, but I waited, so as not to trigger a by-election – I wasn't due to be replaced until May 2017. I spoke to the local Party and the Group Leader about the fact that I did not intend to stand in the next County Council elections which was understood and accepted.

I continued in my capacity of County Councillor, time lapsed and we were asked to consider and vote on the proposed plans for powers to be devolved from Central Government by way of a devolution deal. However, I was aware that this meant we had to have a Mayor for Cambridgeshire and Peterborough, but I did not agree that we needed one.

The Combined Authority (CA) together with a Mayor was yet another tier of government – I would joke and say "It'll all end in tiers!" but it seemed now – if Cambridge City were to get the £70m for housing together with Cambridgeshire and Peterborough getting £100m, we had to have a Mayor.

With this knowledge and having received an email inviting applications for the position of Mayor, I decided this wasn't for me at this time...or was it?!

Given that I wouldn't be a Councillor, the CA would be made up of the leaders from each of the Councils within the relevant authorities – which meant the CA would be all male!

Ummm I thought to myself, Maybe I should put my hat in the ring?!

Apart from this fleeting thought, I hadn't committed much time or thought to the mayoral candidacy.

I don't think I made a conscious planned decision to apply, in fact, I recall being at an event for work (I don't recall the precise event), but I remember it was late, (maybe even as late as 22:30) when I decided I would submit the application! I went into the ladies toilet area, sat on the side and completed the application, sent it electronically, returned to the bar and ordered a drink (probably a soda water and lime).

'What have you done?!' I asked myself whilst waiting for my mandatory cup of ice to crunch alongside my drink, *Was it really the wisest of choices to apply for another political post when my focus was supposed to be returning to legal practice?*

I don't recall precisely how long it was before I found out I'd been shortlisted and selected for interview. I couldn't believe it! The interview was back at Alex Wood Hall, the same place I'd attended when I'd put my hat in the ring for City Councillor candidate.

This time I felt much more relaxed as I waited in the side room, I was called in before the panel following another candidate – there were a few people there to conduct the interview, more than the 5 I'd appeared in front of before and even an MP was here! *Wow.*
I went around the panel and introduced myself, shaking each of their hands. I didn't give a speech on this occasion, this time I answered the questions put to me and maintained eye contact throughout.

It was all smiles and in fact – looking back, I realise matters discussed here, later helped me when campaigning to become the Member of Parliament for Peterborough! But that, unbeknownst to me, was yet to come.

CHAPTER 09

GAME CHANGE?

I received a call shortly after my interview advising I'd been selected as one of the final two candidates. I remember being surprised and in the back of my mind wondering if this was a sign – *should I keep my political hat on?!*

Following my selection I was required to attend husting events at various locations.

The hustings went quite well as I really enjoyed speaking out.

It was one hustings event in particular that stands out in my memory – I remember a gentleman coming up to me at the end and advising me that he had come to support the other candidate, but after hearing me speak – he would not only vote for me – but would help me with anything else I needed!! I couldn't stop smiling – *wow! I felt this was definitely a God connection* – "Thank you so much" I replied. The hustings process came to an end not too long after this event and then I had to wait to find out which of us Party members had chosen to support.

The Christmas holiday period came and went and we were now in 2017. A New Year – a new start!

I don't recall exactly when I heard back but I think it was early 2017. I was at work, when I received the call notifying me that I had missed out to the other candidate by 33 votes. I had obtained 897 votes of support. I explained that this was okay and thanked the caller for letting me know.

As I hadn't been successful I decided my original thoughts of focussing on a legal path made sense, after all I had said to myself that delay is not denial!

Following this thought process, I again reiterated that I wouldn't be standing for re-election and got stuck into looking for other legal vacancies, closer to home.

I recall making contact with a legal recruiter at a recruitment agency I'd used before because they'd been fantastic. I explained that I was looking to go back into a client facing role in a firm closer to home.

The chap I was dealing with asked me to leave it with him, so I was really pleased when he got back in touch advising a firm wished to interview me for the role of Commercial Property Solicitor!

Where I was currently working, my role was to manage a corporate team so was more back office and not client facing at all. I had to look over budgets, consider staff bonuses and meet with the Managing Director – all of which I enjoyed, but I wanted to be more hands on. So this potential new opportunity was exactly that!

The firm was an approximate 20 minute drive from home, no more A14 and there was parking near the office – it seemed perfect!

With that in mind, when I was offered an interview, I accepted. Although I did not inform my current employer that I was actively seeking other positions, it wasn't long after my interview that I was offered the post! Yay!!

I accepted the offer and notified my current place of work, tendered my resignation and began to work my notice.

My notice period was 12 weeks, so when a snap general election was called – my immediate thought was not to try and become a PPC!

By now I was also involved with my local Labour Party and knew that they had a candidate in the 2015 General Election for Peterborough – I had voted for her. Therefore, I had determined that I would seek to be of assistance to her and the campaign if she was to stand again.

Shortly after this, I was asked if I would consider standing in the event that she didn't – I advised that I would, but only if she wasn't, as I'd seen how hard she'd worked for the 2015 campaign, so by rights, she should really have a second bite of the cherry so to speak.

It wasn't long after this discussion that I saw an email inviting self nominations as the previous candidate was not standing....*Gosh* I thought – *I may as well go for it – I have nothing to lose.* Given that I was working my notice period and had accepted a new role, if I was not successful, it would be good practice, I'd learn lots and I'd continue on my legal path – after all - you win or you learn right?

It was almost 02:00 on the date the self-nomination applications closed when I started my application! I kept looking at the responses in the application I'd made for the mayoral candidacy and tried to use those for inspiration – it was late morning by the time I had finished and electronically submitted it. According to the email, this was an open selection and the successful candidate would be notified after the May bank holiday.

It was Tuesday 2 May, I was at work assisting my team when I heard my phone vibrating. I took myself to a vacant office space and answered.

"Hello..., is this Fiona Onasanya?" "Yes, speaking" I replied. The female voice on the other end of the phone explained that Labour would like me to be their PPC in the upcoming elections.

I wanted to scream!
I was so happy – I couldn't quite believe it – I'd been chosen, this was not an all-womens shortlist: this was an open selection, and I'd been chosen!!!!! I thanked the lady for calling to let me know, clasped my hands and tried to stifle my grin.

This was nuts! I was going to stand in the General Election! – Then I had a reality check – *I was going to stand in the upcoming General Election – I need to campaign, oh, but I'm working my notice, and my new employer.... this is a lot* – I need to make some calls and speak to the management.

Although, as I returned to my desk, I could not hide my smile! I asked the managers who were seated behind me if I could have a word. When it was suitably quiet I explained that I had been selected by Labour as their PPC, however, as the constituency of Peterborough had been Conservative for 12½ years, I had never stood in a General Election and I had only lived in Peterborough for nearly 3 years to date, to win was a very big IF!

They explained I would have to speak to HR if I wanted to take time off to campaign and as I was in my notice period – holiday entitlement (if any) would have to be pro rata. "That's okay, I'll go and see HR" I replied.

I practically skipped around to see HR at their side of the office. "I need to take my annual leave entitlement" I advised, explaining it would need to be prorated.
The HR lady got to it straight away, it wasn't too long before she advised my entitlement would be…. Six days.

Six days!!!!?! I thought. As it was a snap election, I only had a little over 5 weeks to campaign!

"Please may I take two of those days off on 8th and 9th June? As 8th is the count itself and polling stations close at 22:00, I don't think I'll have gotten to bed at a decent hour in order to come to work on the 9th!". "That's fine" came the reply. I returned to my desk and continued with my work. At the end of the day after the phone lines had closed and the staff had gone - I emailed my future employers HR dept:

Re: Offer of employment
Tue 02/05/2017 18:27
Hi W,
For your information, as an aside, you may recall in my interview I advised I was standing down as a County Cllr, which I am, but Labour have selected me to be their MP Candidate for Peterborough in the upcoming June elections.
There will be a campaign for the General Election so I wished to let you know as it will be in the press.
Best regards

Fiona

I placed my phone in my bag and shut everything down before making my way to my car. I think I smiled all the way home.

The next day I got up, ready and headed into work – nothing had changed...yet! This was just the beginning!
I got into work super early and checked whether I'd received a reply, I had:

> Thanks for the update Fiona.
> Are you planning to accept if you get elected in?
>
> W

So I replied:

> Hi W,
> If I win the election yes I would, however this is a conservative stronghold so the IF is big!
> Best regards
>
> Fiona

The response I received in reply made me smile and still does!;

> In the nicest possible way, I hope you don't win! ☺
> Keep me posted.
>
> W

They were being so kind to me despite me accepting a position that I might not end up taking, *however that was not what I needed to think about now* – now I needed to learn what was required of me as a PPC!

Apparently I needed an Agent, had to pay for leaflets, pay £500 (which would be refundable in the event I won) and get nominations. 'Phew', I sat back in my chair – *I need to make some calls.*

I went back to work, then on my lunch break, called my cousin. "Cuz!" I said excitedly as he answered, "I need to ask a MASSIVE favour" I continued. He asked how I was doing, (as he always did) and I told him my news explaining that I needed to borrow £500 which I would pay back at the end of June – if not sooner depending on the outcome of the election, "Of course, that would be fine. I'm so so proud of you" he said – "I haven't won yet!" I replied.

Lunch finished and I returned to my desk, having reviewed the email about 'Agents' needing to ring in for a training session – *Agent, who's going to be my Agent as I don't have one?!,* Did I know someone who could help?

Prior to this, I had contacted other people who I knew had also put their hat in the ring for this position, I wanted to offer an olive branch (so to speak) as I'd felt we'd all need to pull together if Labour were to win the seat by me getting elected.

All prospective parliamentary applicants had received my approach well, one of them even offered to attend the meeting with me suggesting they could potentially assist with being an Agent!
Yes! It was all coming together! Or so I thought...Actually, it wasn't! Que comrade!

I recall attending the meeting, there were maybe between 15 to 20 people present. I signed in as an attendee, apologies were given, minutes of the previous meeting circulated (and confirmed as a true and accurate record) then, at matters arising the chair explained I had been chosen and the room applauded, I felt humbled and honoured, thanked everyone and explained I was new to the process and still needed to collate nomination signatures. Now, I don't recall exactly how the next event started, but I recall the person standing and advising they would not be an Agent, nor would they nominate/support my nomination but would ask me to withdraw?!

WTF?! (and not Wow, That's Fantastic!), "What's going on here?!" I asked quizzically. *Never did I think, reaching out, being kind and seeking to be a friend would result in this?!*

I was looked at by the individual with disdain and told "You're not a member of a Trade Union (TU), you should have declared that, had you declared it you wouldn't have been selected.". I was floored! *Why did they wait until now, in front of all these people I didn't know and that didn't yet know me, to say this?!*

"That is simply not true" I responded. "As you know I am a Solicitor and when I sought to join a particular TU previously, I found I couldn't, due to me not working in the public sector. I declared everything in my application and in fact, so as not to further disrupt this meeting, I will email the Regional Director now to see if we can clear up this misunderstanding."

As I sat compiling the email, cc'd to all relevant persons of authority, I glanced up at the disappointed gazes – I couldn't believe this was happening!

The rest of the meeting took place and I departed at it's conclusion. I remember feeling a little bewildered as I drove home. The very next day I saw that a response had been sent to us all:

> Hi all,
>
> The selection panel were aware that Fiona wasn't a member of a TU when they agreed to select her. They have requested that a condition of selection is that candidates join a TU where they are not currently a member of one. Fiona has now joined a TU and has provided confirmation of this.
>
> This matter is now at a close.
>
> Best,

The relief that passed over me reading this was indescribable.

This showed me that everyone applauding your progress is not necessarily happy for you! It is not an act of kindness. No, some people see you as a mosquito – that clap is to kill your desire!

Later that evening I spoke with a lady who has now sadly passed away but was an absolute Godsend! Such a blessing to me and my life, a fountain of knowledge and someone who, in the end, held my hand through this whole process. She reached out after the unfortunate events of the meeting.

I explained that I did not know what an Agent was, what they needed to do and who would (or could) fulfil the role, especially after the person who I thought would help did what they had done.

She reassured me and advised I could leave it with her, she would meet with me at mine and talk me through everything and the steps I would need to be taking.

I was so grateful for this guidance, I felt completely calm and was so happy that I had someone knowledge-able with me in and through this process.

Shortly after this conversation I met with her at mine. She sat with me for a good few hours, taking me step by step, through the process – setting out what I needed to do and areas where she would assist me. She also set about directing me to others who would be of assistance.

Not long after this meeting we met again at my house and she told me she'd not only found me an Agent, but also a person to co-ordinate and arrange my campaign and canvassing dates/schedule!

I recall feeling quite emotional, this lady was doing the most for me, stepping into a void and giving of herself willingly to ensure I had the necessary support and people around me as a team. Now I had progressed from a voice of one to a team of three. Things were now starting to take shape.

Following her guidance it wasn't long before I had my nominations submitted, deposit paid and canvassing dates set, she even sat as the interviewer for my first campaign video!

By this time the campaign was well and truly underway.

I was having to stand and walk lots so had increased my personal training/physio sessions to help me given an historical spinal injury.

The leaflets had been printed and were being delivered – but I'd made another schoolboy error, I'd put my personal number on all the leaflets!! This meant over 40,000 people I didn't know had my number put through their door! *D'oh (facepalm)!*

At first, I hadn't realised this would be an issue as initially I received helpful messages – however, these messages soon became mixed, some offering to help, others asking me if I was lonely and needed a cuddle (yuk!) Or asking if I wanted to meet with them alone, assuring me I could trust they wouldn't hurt me by looking into their eyes! Then there were those individuals who advised that not only did they not like my Party/Party Leader, as I wasn't well known enough I would lose the election!! (constituents)!

My view was – empty barrels make the loudest noise, and what naysayers thought of me was none of my business! So this flurry of messages was soon forgotten as the polling day drew ever closer!

At work I'd asked if I could take the rest of my prorated holiday entitlement as half days (as I'd been leaving home at 06:00, going in early, working a full day, travelling back to Peterborough after work to campaign, then going from there to Cambridge for gym and physio!). It was a lot!

The volunteers that the Campaign Manager had been gathering had been a tremendous help. We had not had help centrally and the secretary had been seconded to assist with the Cambridge seat, as the retention of that seemed to take precedence. That didn't matter now though, as today was the day!

Polling day was finally here!!

I got up super early (despite not having work), I had to get ready and head to the polling station! Today's vote would be for me by me! I drove to my polling station and spoke to the volunteers collecting data.

The plan was to vote, then go to visit the various stations and committee rooms and thank everyone for standing with and supporting me today.

I drove around to all polling stations and spoke to the helpful volunteers that were collating data. Everyone was smiley – I even bumped into the sitting MP who wished me luck!

After visiting the other people assisting me I decided it made sense to call it a day and finally get some food. I called mum, she was meeting me at mine, I agreed we'd get something ordered in (if in doubt, eat out!) So we agreed on a chinese.

I spoke to my Campaign Manager via the walkie-talkie app he'd set up on my phone (it was so much fun!) and headed home.

On arrival I parked up, mum was already there waiting "Mummy!" I exclaimed as I wrapped my arms around her - she smiled.

We went inside and I filled her in on the days events. It was now late – I said we should go and pick up some food – "Ummm why don't we grab some special fried rice? There's a chinese round the corner – we can come back here to eat." So we drove together to get some food, when we got back we put on the repeat of a talent show and ate.

Gosh, is that the time?!, I looked at the time and went upstairs to get ready. I came back downstairs in my bargain red dress (it cost £7 from a charity shop!) and heels.

Mum turned to look at me, we held hands and prayed.

"Right let's go" she said.   As I stepped out of the door I turned and said "Mum, when I set foot back over this threshold, it will be as the MP for Peterborough!", "According to your faith, so be it!" came the scriptural reply.

Mum drove us to the East of England Arena – the Stanground Showground. I had to show my invitation to security, then we were shown where to park.

Once parked we went through security, our bags were checked and we were given wristbands.

There was the buzz of excitement and anticipation in the air. As mum and I wandered around the various tables we could see people counting, others watching, people talking, and the media seeking to speak with the candidates.

I was asked if I would be willing to speak to a reporter, to which I obliged. "Did you see the exit polls?" "Exit polls? No we got a chinese and watched a talent show on repeat!" The reporter looked stunned.

I don't recall whether I had any further questions put to me but I remember shortly thereafter we went into the Main Hall. I sat down with mum *(as I'd worn heels!)* and waited.

It was approximately 1am when the Returning Officer called us to the table. *Where is my Agent?* A tannoy was put out summoning him. Once we were all present the spoilt ballots were shown and explained to us all before the sitting MP and I were advised that the numbers were close! *Oh my!!* His Agent requested that the bundles of votes be checked and it was agreed that the piles would be flicked through. The counting therefore continued until 3am. Shortly thereafter I was invited to come up to the podium together with the other candidates as the results were read out...

"Onasanya Fiona Oluyinko (sic) Labour Party 22,950"

Cheers erupted!

After the crowd had quietened down it was declared that I had been duly elected the Member of Parliament for Peterborough and I was invited to speak:

"Thank you everyone!" I put my hands together, clasped and looked upwards in appreciation to God: "First of all I'd just like to say thank you and thank you to you all, I'm so grateful for you choosing to make a choice for change, we've made our choice, now let's make the change – thank you!"

I stepped back in line and shook hands with the other candidates. *This is it, I am now the MP for Peterborough!!!*

There were lots of camera flashes and reporters vying for my attention, after interviews and pictures I exited the Showground with mum "My feet are broken, note to self, never wear heels to a count!" I mumbled through my grin to mum.

We went back to mine and the adrenaline was still pumping around my body! *I'm the MP, I'm the MP!!!*

We got in, I kicked off my shoes, put on the election results and switched off my phone (which was flooded with congratulatory messages and WhatsApp's).

By now it was after 6am on the Friday! I decided to clamber into bed. I was so grateful and smiling, I drifted off to sleep.

Later that day I woke up turned on my phone and as the messages flooded in I received the following email:

Subject: congratulations!
Importance: High

Dear Fiona

Many congratulations on your successful election to the MP for Peterborough. It wasn't such a big 'IF' after all.

May we clarify your position in terms of _____? I assume from your exchange of emails with W that you expect to be working full time as an MP and will not be able to take up the position that we have offered. Is that the case? It will be disappointing for us but we fully understand your ambition and political commitment

Best regards

Oh gosh, yes of course, I need to contact work! I emailed my employer and explained that due to the exceptional circumstance of the election win, I would not be able to return and work the remainder of my notice, *I start in Parliament on Monday!*

CHAPTER 10

LET'S BEGIN!

I set off early, expectant,
excited and cautiously optimistic!
I wonder what it will be like?!

As I board the underground and look around at the commuters, I can't help but grin with excitement. *I'm going to Westminster – the actual Palace of Westminster!!!*

As I get off with my little suitcase – I gaze up the escalators smiling. *I've arrived!*

Inside the Palace was like a maze!!! I remember being star struck at seeing MP's in person that I'd only ever seen on TV! Getting lost, picking up my laptop, iPad and being given lots of freebies just like a Freshers Fair when you go to Uni!

I'd been appointed a buddy to help me navigate through Parliament and the process, then I was introduced to the doorkeepers! They were awesome! Any difficulties you experienced, they were there to assist with and always at hand if you were in need of guidance or in my case sweets!!

Over time I built a great rapport with them and even had pet names for my favorites (shout out Shoog, Jugs, Monty, Minnie, KP, Icey, Matt the drummer, Fittie, Bert, Ernie, Sweetie, Daddy Cool, The Joker, Wonder Wayne and Ness to name but a few!). They could always be found in a lobby, committee corridors, behind the Speaker's chair or outside the library.

I remember walking into the library and thinking this was breath taking grandeur!
We had several inductions over the following days and weeks but a cataclysmic crisis occurred on the Wednesday of the week I was beginning to settle in; that catastrophic event was Grenfell Tower fire.

This avoidable catastrophe which should have never happened troubled me. It just didn't make sense. Why were the Government seemingly dragging its feet? When would a Judge be appointed so the public inquiry could start? Was the cladding on the building compliant with building regulations? These questions still remained unanswered, so the following week on 21 June 2017 I bobbed and asked my first Prime Ministers Question (PMQ) – despite not yet having made my Maiden speech.

I didn't feel scared or nervous – answers were needed!
I was stunned at how flustered and flummoxed the response I received came across. *What's going on here?!*

This was a regular occurrence. I am a very results oriented person but the machine of government can be quite slow at moving towards results and in my opinion, often struggles to keep up with the pace of societal developments.

On July 5 2017 I subsequently made my Maiden speech and then had to get to hiring staff, finding and setting up a constituency office, tackling constituency matters, attending functions, events and speaking engagements, reading up on parliamentary procedures and protocols, reviewing and responding to emails, conducting surgeries and that was just the start!

I had also been appointed to the Select Committee for Communities and Local Government, as well as being asked to become a Private Parliamentary Secretary for the Shadow Defence Minister prior to recess.

We returned to Parliament in the Autumn and I was excited – *this would be my first budget!* Plus, now I could really get my teeth into the roles to which I'd been appointed.

My contribution to the budget was of particular significance and a noteworthy part of my journey as it went viral!!

But this was just the beginning. In a matter of months, my name was about to become a matter of interest and widely known by the public – not because of my appointment to the whips office, no, it would be for the charge of 'Doing an act tending and intended to pervert the course of public justice.' Something which I stated back then and maintain now, that I did not do.

In the May of 2018 I was at home when I was served with a written requisition mandating me to appear before Westminster Magistrates Court on 28 June 2018. However, this date was subsequently changed to 12 July. In July, I appeared before the Magistrates court to enter my plea - *Not Guilty.*

Parliament did not rise until some 12 days later on 24 July. Thankfully, it was the day after this that the media storm ensued.

On 13 August 2018, I appeared before the Old Bailey to re-enter my plea; *Not Guilty,* and a trial date was set for 12 November 2018.

A week or so before the commencement of the November trial, I was advised that my brother, was changing his plea. He had actually provided false details on this and 2 other occasions in order to avoid losing his licence. Armed with this information coupled with the fact my licence was (and still is) clean, the CPS were asked to drop the charge against me now matters had become clear. I had to wait to see if this would be the end of this horrendous saga. Sadly it was not, as they refused – the trial was set for 5 days, but it lasted 11, a member of the jury asked if they could be discharged so a jury of 12 became that of 11 and they did not reach a verdict. With a hung jury, the CPS requested a re-trial. The re-trial commenced some 15 days later – every article and news report I came across asserted that I was guilty – *despite the fact my brother had changed his plea, explaining what he'd done.*

CHAPTER 11

GAME OVER?

Aguilty verdict was returned after my re-trial. I sat quietly. *How can you be innocent yet found guilty? How?* Wow. This is not how I imagined it would be – I honestly thought I would be acquitted or found not guilty – these were the only two options I had considered.

The burden of proof is on the prosecution but it seems inconsistencies and lack of motive have not been borne in mind. Despite the Judge agreeing that having read the evidence and character statements this is totally out of character; Despite my brother owning up (eventually with a change in Solicitors) to providing false information and despite my explanations numerous times; the jury offered a guilty verdict – I do not accept this.

Nonetheless, as it was December of 2018, I would have to return in January to be sentenced.

Prior to this situation *I had faith in justice.* I honestly believed if you are innocent – you need not worry; after all, worry is a misuse of your imagination! However, I have realised that sometimes, just like my thoughts years before when the London riots happened, there is no justice – *it 'just-is'!*

My thinking was that there must be some rationale or reason for all of this. *I know the Bible says His ways are not our ways but this was WILD!*

It's a strange feeling – you can't focus on anything being said – you have people looking at you and as I would later learn, this was common practice!

Yet, to share a Fiona-ism about my circumstances – I kept telling myself that like a battery you need positive and negative to work, *God must have a plan in all of this.*

CHAPTER 12

SENTENCED

I t's Tuesday 29th January 2019 and my sentencing hearing is at 10am. Usually I'm up early anyway but it's 4:50am, I decide to get up, showered and my usual cup of ice! (I love to crunch ice cubes).

I call my mum for an ETA - *it's now 6am and she should be arriving anytime now.* Mum advises she's only just leaving hers – so I layback and listen to "Intentional" by Travis Greene *(The words are very apt! ☺).* Ever since the trial/re-trial, my knowing that the court opens at 8am and the fact that the press are not always as many at that time; I seek to get there early, after all to be early is be on time and to be on time is to be late *(which ironically I usually am!)* But today it seems we won't get there early - *not that it matters – we have time.*

Mum arrives – she smiles but looks concerned, I tell her not to worry - *God's got me* – I look at the time, gosh! It's 8am – then I smile imagining all the press waiting to pounce – but I'm not there!

As it's rush hour we miss 3 undergrounds before there is sufficient space for us to get on. Sunglasses (or "Pap-shades" as mum calls them) are conveniently on my head as well as earmuffs! (The latter are because it's chilly). We get to our designated place and hail a taxi. I go through the usual – *"Please can you take us to The Old Bailey, there will probably be lots of press – so apologies in advance – I will need to get as close to the doors as possible, mum, don't forget your shades."* "I've got my brolly too" she replies. *She is always prepared yet prayerful - looking out for and after me.* Mum likens the media to "Hounds hunting" which although banned as a barbaric sport, these "Hounds" have cameras and legal licence to hunt!

It reminds me of the re-trial, after the verdict there was a press scrum and out of nowhere came this black brolly – pow! – for that reason I called mum, Mary Poppins!

We pull up outside the Court – the press presence can be clearly seen, flashes of cameras and a number of reporters surround the cab – mum places £10 in the tray and I thank the driver, the door opens and mum steps out, I remind myself not to smile and step out...

"Miss Onasanya" some shout, others are just focused on me, determined to get the "Money shot." There are so many I am struggling to get through, I see a gap! But at the same time mum seeks to guide me and moves me away from the space. I move her hand from my back and lose sight of the space - *damn!* All the while remembering not to react - *that's what those with cameras want,* so poker face it is!

A kind security lady appears from behind the media scrum "Can you let her through please" she shouts – the press are still surrounding me, blocking the entrance – "Can you stop and let her through" she shouts again. From nowhere, over my head a brolly opens – *mum* I think to myself – I push it out of my face and enter the Court – I made it!

Now the wait begins.

To be fair it's not too early so my legal team should arrive any time now I think to myself. "Fiona" I hear, I look up, "Hey, hi, have you been waiting long?" "No, I've been here 5/10 minutes max" I smile. *The press probably got here early so I bet they're really chilly!* – this thought makes me smile to myself.

Shortly after this I'm asked whether I got caught up in the press scrum as they are now "Wise to my trick" of arriving early – I chuckle as I reply "I wasn't early this morning."

We make our way upstairs. It's different this time, usually we go to the room, but not today. Today there is no room. Counsel greets us and directs us to be seated at a table.

We all take a seat but before Counsel can get into the detail, a reporter comes over and asks if I have any comment to make about the appeal? "No" I reply.

"She does not wish to make any comment at this time" my Solicitor interjects.
The reporter turns to leave and I roll my eyes. My Solicitor gives me a reassuring smile and then Counsel proceeds.
I don't recall much that was said – my thoughts and focus are turned towards the sentencing.

CHAPTER 13

COURT 1

O ver the tannoy I hear "All parties in the case of Onasanya to Court 1, all parties in Onasanya to Court 1.". I stand and inhale, *This is it.*

The court room is different, there is what looks like a glass box in the centre of the room, I can't see mum – *I can't see anyone up in the public gallery?*

People are looking at me, *Journalists?* There are quite a few people in the courtroom - it's a different layout to that of my trials so I'm not sure who's where.

My Solicitor asks if I'm okay, I advise I am and ask where I go as the door to the dock was locked and no dock officer was present. I remove my overcoat and fold it over my arms – *is it just me or is it really hot in here?*

I enter the dock and am joined by my brother. Our names are confirmed and we are directed to take a seat on the front bench. *This feels so different.*

I stared out from behind the glass panels – the Judge was yet to come in, I recognised the clerk but was distracted by other people in the room. My brother was seated to my right, he too was facing forward.

This felt so surreal, I can't see mum who's been through two trials with me, she (as well as my belief and trust in God) has been my rock, yet the person I can see – the reason why I'm here, is seated beside me.

I have often said that unforgiveness is like pinching yourself expecting the other person to experience pain – so I can't explain what this is that I feel – is it hate? Anger? Hurt? I don't know – I'm just questioning how this can be justice? Concerned for how mum must be feeling, seeing both her children sitting in the dock and wondering what is going on in Fes's head. He's always brushed stuff off – but I know he has a big heart and never would have intended to hurt others or myself by making such a massive error of judgement. He had apologised and explained the rationale behind his decision to me - we'd both shed tears as I knew he'd not intended for this to come back on anyone, let alone me and he was truly sorry but I, as a result, was on the brink of losing everything over and above my liberty. So sitting here, I was just numb.

The vacant space in my minds eye was abruptly disrupted as I heard "All rise..."

CHAPTER 14

SENT DOWN

It seemed like forever that the Judge was asking questions of the prosecution. The CPS QC seemed to delight in yet again rehearsing matters – I sat in silence screaming in my mind "I DID NOT LIE TO THE POLICE!!!" but what did it matter now, the press had painted a picture and the public bought into it. No-one cared that the signature was not my own, nor the fact that I did not return false information, what mattered now was that a jury had found me guilty and I had to be sentenced on that basis.

I recall feeling like I did at trial – I stared at the Judge – not daring to look at anyone else so I could not be accused of trying to intimidate or look at anyone in any type of way!
I must have zoned out but I came to when the Judge was asking my QC if she could help direct him.

It sounded to me like he was asking whether there was any reason why he should not serve me with an immediate custodial sentence – a copy of my medical information detailing the diagnosis of Multiple Sclerosis was handed up.

Meanwhile, I was sitting here watching my private health information played out in public. *I guess a life in the public eye means personal details will be shared publicly.*

The Judge appeared to be listening intently, he set out what he thought he was going to be doing explaining that he would retire to consider deliberations made and then hand down the sentence.

The court were asked to rise and the Judge retired.
I sat back down and enquired of the dock officer what happens now? My brother interjected "We can leave now" I looked at the dock officer and she agreed "Yes you can leave the dock, but you cannot leave the building."

My legal team were waiting on the outside of the dock for me "Are you okay?" I was asked. I quietly nodded.

We went to wait on the bench outside the courtroom and I sat drinking a cup of hot water as my brother waltzed past smiling – I frowned, *how could he be smiling and so casual, when this was such a serious situation?!* My QC and Solicitor saw my bemused expression and as if I could read their minds, I retorted "It's absolutely fine, this is how he is, so laid back he's horizontal!"

They looked shocked. By this time I'd resolved in myself that to worry would indeed be a misuse of my imagination as this whole situation had unfolded in the opposite way that I had supposed – much like life really!

The current President of the United States was unexpected, much like the fact I'd become an MP at 33 years old in a marginal seat, I'd been found guilty of a crime I did not commit and I had never realised certain people would come to court and behave as they did.

Evidence shared verbally differed so dramatically from the papers, *why did they hate me so much?!* As I let my mind run away with those thoughts and questions I heard my surname over the tannoy again – it was time to go back.

I went back through to Court 1, back into the dock, back down the steps to be searched out of the view of prying eyes and then took a seat for my fate to be sealed through sentencing.

We all rose for the return of the Judge.

I remember the passing down of the judgement, first my brother was asked to stand, now it was my turn.
As I stood I looked straight out to the Judge, the words seem muffled, I have no words, no thoughts, I just listen as the Judge advises I'm going to prison – an immediate custodial sentence of 3 months.
Take them down.

CHAPTER 15

CELLS

My brother and I are lead down the stairs. He keeps telling me I'll be okay. I'm lead along concrete corridors and taken to an area where I am asked questions, I have to hand over the few belongings I have, I am then searched again and handcuffed. I'm taken past a number of holding cells to the cell with the open door. *This is my holding cell,* I'm shown in, the cuffs are removed and the door is closed and locked.

This cell is a small room beneath the Old Bailey.
Literally speaking, it comprised of a wooden bench in-between exposed brickwork that had been painted with no heat.

I take a seat on the wooden bench, there is a newspaper on the bench, but it's not today's. *I wonder how today will be reported.*

As I unfold the paper, the hatch opens and the door unlocks. I'm told I have a legal visit?!
I am taken out from the holding cell - I distinctly remember being led past people either trying to peer out through their cell hatch, or seeking to get an officers attention, ironic really as prison is similar but much louder.

I'm taken to an area where I am told to put on an orange tabard, I am walked along past a set of rooms to a vacant one, seated and the cuffs are once again removed from my wrist.

I rub my hand over the wrist which was cuffed as my legal team enter. There are apologies that we are where we are and explanations of what happens next. I am going to prison – probably Bronzefield.

But here I am, smiling. As Phyllis Diller said – "A smile is a curve that sets everything straight!" I say to my Solicitor, "God must want my path to cross with someone there." Mentally I am expectant and calm?!

Looking back, I think my faith is the reason why I felt expectant and calm because I had a belief deep down in my soul that this, although it didn't make sense, was one part of a bigger picture.

My team leave and I am returned to the holding cell to be left in solitude until the hatch opens again – I'm asked if I want food – *gosh I haven't eaten at all today, I should eat something.* I explain I don't eat meat but will eat everything else – bar mushrooms! (Yuk!)

Food was brought to me in my cell and I began eating the hot microwave meal. I had just finished it when I was told a gentleman from Probation was waiting to speak to me, *Probation?! Why?*

I was collected, cuffed and lead back along the concrete corridor, the tabard was placed back on and I was lead to a waiting room. I sat quietly in the room waiting, *this is so surreal.*
A gentleman came in introducing himself and advised that he needed to go through some questions and a form with me.

This reminded me of the pre-sentence report meeting after the verdict was returned (prior to the date I had to return for sentencing). I again repeated that I had not done that which I had been subsequently convicted of and was advised my level of risk was deemed low having not ever offended before. *Before?! I have never offended!! I accept not completing or returning the form – but this innocent mistake is not what I stood accused of and indeed subsequently convicted.*

Following our discussion and the completion of his form with me I was returned to the holding cell.

It was around 6pm when I was taken back out of my cell, cuffed and walked along the concrete corridor again. This time there was no tabard, I was taken past this area to a waiting vehicle. *This must be the prison bus. I mean I know it's not a bus but this is the closest comparator I had.*

There were steps onto the bus, the officer on board asked that my cuffs be removed. A door was opened to my right aboard the bus. Behind it was a small compartment, I was told to go in and sit on the box, *this must be what is called a sweatbox.* There is no seatbelt but there is a small window to my left, the surface in front of me slopes inwards by my feet and straight up in front of my face. The door to this area is locked with me inside.

I look out of the window, this looks like a depot area, I can hear other people getting on amongst the jingle jangle of keys. The engine starts and we are on our way...but to where? *I know I'm going to prison, but which one? Oh yes, the Solicitor said probably Bronzefield because of the court I was in, the probation chap said I'm "low risk" so I'll just have wait to see.*

As we passed people I couldn't help but think back to my younger girlie holiday days, where you would be driven to a particular holiday resort, you'd never been to before, no one is bothered by the coach or your presence, life simply carries on around it, no one knows or cares that you are there, you are just anonymous.

The cacophony of noise has subsided, there are no flashing cameras, no phone pinging with messages, just me looking out at passers by living their daily lives doing business as usual.

I drift off to sleep. I think a couple of hours have passed, the driver is listening to Smooth FM, ironically "Time of my Life" is playing as we pull up – I try to peer out but it's dark and rainy. The officer opens the hatch and explains that we have to be checked in individually so I will have to stay seated and wait a little while, but I've arrived.

It wasn't too long before my door was unlocked and I was handcuffed to the officer to disembark. Once off the bus I was escorted into the building.

CHAPTER 16

THE START

I am greeted by a friendly officer who advises I will need to see the Dr/Nurse. I ask if I can use the toilet *I'm desperate!* I'm told I can, just as soon as I've been checked in.

The nurse weighs me, *shouldn't I take my shoes off?* 66 kilos he says – I work in stones and pounds so I figure it's around 10 stone, *I'm sure I'm 11,* he asks me lots of questions including whether I'm pregnant – *absolutely not unless it's the immaculate conception, what time would I have had to conceive?!* Following our discussion he also enquires whether I take drugs or drink alcohol – "No", I reply.

"Spice" he enquires, *Spice? All the time! I think to myself.* "Yes, every time" I reply. "That's illegal even though it's a legal high." *What?! I meant spice like seasoning, salt and pepper!!.* Bewildered I get up and ask again if I may use the toilet. I am shown to the ladies, *phew finally.* There's a door that someone could see over if they came close – my legs can be seen beneath.

After I wash my hands I am taken into the hallway where I'm met by another officer, she has really kind eyes and is really nice. She introduces herself, *that's my cousins name!* We take a seat in a room and I am asked whether I have ever been abused, self harm or have thoughts of suicide? Wow! I advise that the answer to all three of those questions is no but ask "What if I had experienced abuse or answered yes?" I'm told someone would see me the following day. *So a Pandora's box would be opened, then you would be shown to a cell alone?! Goodness me!*

I express my surprise and we conclude our discussion, I sign my form, have my photo and fingerprints taken and am brought to the main desk. I am informed I will be shown to the induction wing, asked if I have anything I shouldn't and I'm given a list to check. I remember I have sanitary towels tucked into my boot (as I didn't have a bag). "I don't think so, but I have a brace in my boot to aide my walking and these" I reply as I put the towels on the side. "Oh, you can't have these" came the reply as the lady took my towels! *You can't have sanitary towels?!* "Why?" I ask, explaining that I was expecting to come on, but the lady explains there are prison issue towels. "Do they have wings? as I am quite heavy." The lady advises they don't. *But what if I leak?!*

I am taken to be searched again and asked to remove my boots. I ask for a seat as the boot with my brace takes some pulling! As I take my boot off the officer looks horrified – I tell her not to worry and remove the brace so it can be examined – "This is why I walk funny" I explain. After I'm patted down I am shown back through to the reception area.

Another prisoner is there, she gives me a white netted bag of items – a plastic knife, fork and spoon. A plastic plate, bowl and mug, two flasks, a toothbrush, toothpaste, a small bar of soap, conditioner, shampoo, 2 grey tracksuit bottoms, 2 grey t-shirts, a jumper, nightie, 3 pairs of black socks and 6 knickers. *I remember being shown these bags when I visited HMP Peterborough in my capacity as MP.*

I am advised that I can make a call, I ask to ring my mum – I knew her number and they gave me a pin. I tried to call but there was no answer – I am told I can try again so this time I leave a voicemail advising where I am and leaving details of my prison number.

I am then shown to my house block, this spur is the induction wing. It's approaching 9pm so everyone is behind their doors. I'm shown up to the top landing, to a cell which is unlocked, I am told to go inside, the door is locked behind me and the hatch closed. I sit on the corner of the bed. The mattress is one of those plastic covered ones like a floor mat you would use in a gym class at school but this is not as thick.

There is a sheet, one pillow and a thin blanket, the toilet and sink are right beside the door. The privacy screen shields the toilet from the cell but an officer would be able to look through the hatch and see you. No part of the cell is hidden. There is a television on the side so I am able to use it to listen to the radio. There is no curtain so the light over the courtyard shines into my cell and there is also a telephone – but I cannot use it as I had not be allocated my pin.

I set about putting my bag to one side, changing into my nightie and brushing my teeth, *where do I shower? I have no moisturiser!*

I sit on the bed, *I guess this is me - it's not too bad, I have my own cell, the lady checking me in seemed nice, the officers were friendly...*I begin reading through the information in the envelope I'd been given. I find a Christian radio station via the TV – they are talking about me!

I close the book and lay back listening to the presenters passing judgement (as opposed to praying) and making comments. *I listen but the report becomes a blur as I drift off to sleep.*

CHAPTER 17

PRISON

I wake up super early - it's only just after 1am – I lay there in darkness.

It was 5:15am before I got up, I know they don't unlock you until 8am (that's what the booklet said) so I did my teeth, put the radio on and started reading.

It is always important to remember that we do not have to be imprisoned in mind despite a physical setting.

Questions remain unanswered and appeals yet to be determined.

When the Judge was sentencing me, he made reference a number of times to "The Office I am privileged to hold." He said that "No special consideration would be given to me" but this seems extraordinary because, if I wasn't in this position, *would I have had the Recorder of London presiding over the trial? Would I have had a re-trial some 15 days later? Would I then have had a High Court Judge in the Central Criminal Court (The Old Bailey)? Would I have been prosecuted by a QC?, served a written requisition by a murder detective and officer with a body cam? As well as having the Serious Organised Crime Agency (SOCA) involved?! I personally think the answer is no!*

All of these very important people and agencies for me.....however, I think special consideration has already been given, quite ironically, because of "The Office I am privileged to hold."

I am presently, in prison....according to the news (radio) "A number" of people have written to the Attorney General complaining my sentence is too lenient: *too lenient?!*...this astounds me.

I am not sure how my seeking to appeal the conviction, getting sentenced (despite the bid to appeal against conviction pending) **and having my liberty removed** – *thus becoming detained;* is too lenient?! Personally I feel that sentencing should have only taken place in the event my appeal bid failed – *how is this just?!*

A voice interrupts my train of thought. "Morning" shouts the voice from the other side of the door as it was unlocked and pushed open. "Morning." It was 8:10am, I made my way down the stairs from my landing – ladies were beginning to queue for breakfast. I remember thinking to myself whilst looking out at everyone; *this is like walking into a supermarket – lots of people, not all female but as you watch them*

leafing through magazines, dawdling though isles, looking at
shelves – you have no idea who they are, why they're there,
what's going on in their minds, what they did before coming
there or what they are capable of!
I went to queue and realised everyone had their plastic
bowl, plate and cutlery – I left the queue and returned to my
cell to collect mine.

I went back down to join the queue, looking at all these
women – they all seemed ordinary, I looked around taking
in my environment – "Miss" the loudness of the title gets
my attention, I look in the direction of the call and point
to myself, the officer nods and points towards the server.
"Cereal? Toast?" "May I have some rice krispies please"
I reply, the elderly looking lady scoops a mug full and pours
it into my bowl. She then hands me a small plastic carton
of semi-skimmed milk. "Oh, sorry I don't drink cows milk. I
use almond milk at home, I guess I could try soya if there's
no almond?" The server looks at me like I've lost my mind!!
"This ain't Costa" I'm ushered along.

I take a seat at the tables – they look like the tables you
get in school, there are plastic chairs but there are only
a few other inmates seated here. "You're new ain't ya?"
one says. "Yes I arrived last night" I reply. "You'll be fine
babes" another girl chips in, "Don't worry, the first night's
the worst."

They all seem so ordinary.
I engage in light conversation and then we are told to get
behind our doors. It's 9am, we are locked up until noon. At

lunchtime the doors are unlocked again, I go down with my plate and cutlery this time. As I queue up a couple of the girls I spoke to at breakfast come over. There is chit chat and I get served lunch, I can't remember what it was but I must have looked at it strangely as one of the girls took one look at my face and asked if I knew how to order menu choices. *Menu choices? You get menu choices in prison?!*

I get taken over to the pod, I have to place my index finger onto the centimetre wide pad for my index finger to be read. The inmate shows me how to make my food choices for the next week. Just as we finish, the same command "Behind your doors ladies" is made so I make my way back to my cell as we now have to be locked up until dinner.

At dinner time I'm let out again, before queuing up I go back to the pod to print my movement slip – *I have my induction starting tomorrow at 08:55.*

I queue up for my evening meal, remarking on how nice the server and everyone had been. As we sit down I enquire why and for how long one of the ladies were in for? "Babes, if I were you, I wouldn't ask so many questions, never ask why someone's here, like what they did and what they got - you're new so I'll allow you, oh and her...she's in for murdering her 3 grandchildren, torching their bodies and setting them as stakes on her garden fence."

That information made me internalize my thoughts: *Oh my goodness – where on earth have I been sent?!*

Shortly thereafter I learnt that this prison housed Category A offenders, Rosemary West had been here, lifers were usually on a particular House Block, there was even a House Block for detoxing "Nitties" (drug addicts).

That evening as I lay in my cell I couldn't help but think looks can be deceiving! Everyone seems so ordinary – I drifted off wondering how long I would be here.

I slept a little better that night, I could still feel the metal base through the mattress against my hip which felt a little bruised and the light still came in through the window, but at least I had a single cell.

The next morning was the same unlock time but this time I had inductions – yay! At least I wouldn't be locked up, I can meet my Caseworker and the prison Chaplain.

I had been permitted to try and call my mum again but *still no answer* so I had given the prison caseworker her number. I then had to take tests to determine my level of Maths and English, followed by questions on cleaning and food safety. I returned to my wing and met with the Chaplain who was lovely. I asked for a Bible and was told I had to use the pod to order one but I could attend the 'Women of Destiny' weekly Bible studies, Evening Praise and Sunday morning services.

My faith is so important to me so to have the ability to participate in collective worship showed me that although I had been locked up, God could not be locked out!

In my Maiden speech I had said that I was a woman of faith and liked acronyms, so my acronym for faith was For All In This House, however, now this acronym had become Forsaking All I Trust Him.

My faith kept me focused.

It was now lunchtime so I went back downstairs to queue. "Onasanya, clear your cell, you're moving." I look over at the extremely tall loud male officer, *I'm moving? Where? Now? How come?.* "What's happened, can I get lunch?" I enquire. I'm told that I can eat but I have to be fast as I will be collected in 15 mins!

I didn't have much as I had only come into prison in the clothes I stood up in at Court, it had only been 2 days so I hadn't really taken much out of the bag. I ate my bagel with the teaspoon of peanut butter wrapped in cling film that they had given me and went to my cell to gather my belongings.

As I came back down I went over to wait by the metal bars. "Where's your bedding?" an officer asks. "Bedding?!" *the bed was made when I arrived so I left it back as I found it.*

I explained this to the officer and she asked me to go back and retrieve the bedding. I went back, stripped the bed and as I came back down she advised I'd need to leave the sheets, pillow cases and duvet cover, so back I went. I came down for the third time and she said I should have left the quilt – "I'm sorry but I'm not going back up again, anything that needs to be returned will have to be taken from here."

I'd had enough of hobbling up and down stairs, traipsing items up and down and by this time, was extremely hot!

I was stood with my bag and bedding by the gate when an officer came with a list, I had to show my card and confirm my name, another lady had since come to the gate with her stuff – but she had several clear plastic bags. The officer asked us to follow him, I asked where we were going. "You're moving as this is just the induction" *oh gosh, we're going to general population – but it won't be that bad, I thought to myself, after all, I've seen how this is.*

As we cross over to a different wing of the same House Block I can hear a woman screaming "OFFICER!!!!" the bars are unlocked, opened, we're let through, they're closed and locked behind us. *The clang of the gate and rustling of the keys I can still hear in my mind now!*

We are shown to a cell – together. *I'm sharing.* The lady I am placed in the cell with does not have a very good command of English.

Through broken English I try to explain that due to my leg I need to be on the bottom bunk please – she looks puzzled "I no share."

After some back and forth with my explaining that she has to share with me, *it's not optional!* She begins to put her bags on the shelf and I set about doing the same. *Am I safe? Is she aggressive? How long has she been here? Why is she here?* Are all questions which raced through my mind.

I needn't have had concerns though, my cell mate, who I will call B was safe, she could be abrupt, especially loud when conversing and brash – partly due to culture but mainly due to her frustration of being in prison which I understand. I mean, *how do you share what this feels like?*

No privacy, male officers able to look through your hatch anytime they feel/deem it necessary, knocking and entering without awaiting a response when you may be getting changed or even naked following a shower – and you share a cell, so you could be on the toilet - which has no door, so she hears, sees and indeed smells what's happening and speaks to you whilst she is straining on the loo!!!

I think it is both exceptional and extraordinary to see and experience the justice system from this side of the door (so to speak), especially when I know I am blessed to be in a role where I can offer practical assistance to many of these ladies.

There are so many stories, experiences and events that I have heard, come across and partaken of and I'm not even a week in!

As time passed we became friends - in fact in prison, you have no concept of the days/weeks because they all roll into one, relationships forge quickly but those comrade/constituent personalities show through because a mask can only be worn for so long.

You soon learn who the snakes are, who the hustlers are, the trouble makers, those who consider themselves "Studs" and those who just want to keep their heads down.

I can't recall the exact day when we were sitting on the landing (there were chairs on the landing outside of our cell). I think it was over lunch when I was asked what I thought about G4S. "Well I think public and private should be kept separate, intermingling the two sectors causes profit to take precedence over people I feel." The lady looks at me absolutely baffled, "What are you on about?" "G4S" I reply, "like Serco and Sodexo, I know it says HMP but the prisons are run by private companies." A roar of laugher erupted; "Nah babes, G4S is Gay 4 the Stay."

If I could have gone red, I'm sure I would have! "Ohhhh, No I'm not" "So you're strictly?" *Now given my G4S blunder I didn't want to make any assumptions about what 'strictly' meant* "What's strictly as the only strictly I have heard of is the dancing competition" "Strictly dickly" came the reply.

I couldn't believe how forward these ladies were – I was a total stranger! "Yes, if that means I like males" I replied.
I think it was possibly day 12, I'd completed my inductions, received my food safety certificate, established that I had passed all exams and been appointed a wing cleaner. My cell mate would collect our breakfast so I could ensure I got in and out of the shower first thing and she would shower when I was cleaning, as our cell would be unlocked.

On this particular day I had been in the shower when I heard a fracas – the shower was like swimming pool showers, you press a button and as soon as the button releases, the water stops. There are 2 showers and 1 bath for all of us to use on the top landing and the same is available for use on the bottom landing. Toilets are within your cell. The water had ceased so I wrapped my towel around me and exited to return to my cell across the landing.

A lady had come out of the shower, without her towel, so stark naked and still wet. She was dancing using the mop as a pole. *What is going on here?!* Officers were shouting "Behind your door!" as she stood shaking her naked derrière.

I was flabbergasted, it seemed this was perfectly normal, some ladies chatted whilst others laughed – *"I'm not involved"* I mutter as I walk straight across the landing to my cell and push the door to.

This was just one of many incidents! The ladies could be quite forward!! So it was very much a learning curve for me. I recall having a visit from my mum, she'd sent in some clothes so I'd made an effort to change out of the tracksuit into a cardigan and my skinny jeans but the response from some women was worse than what I imagine walking onto a building site in a bikini would rouse!!

I even recall hearing "Do you take f#¿» in your bottom?"...it was a lot.

In addition to this you had the measly meals – one such meal was a plate of spaghetti hoops! I even recall being told to smell milk – it was out of date – but we were advised it smelt fine so was good to use!

All of this was in addition to the screaming & shouting, officers ignoring the fact you were ringing your buzzer and ladies who were mentally unwell banging and screaming like whaling banshees in the early hours.

I quickly learned that not all officers cared and most appeared to be male – which surprised me as this was a female establishment?!
As time progressed not only did my cell mate open up to me, she told me she had been imprisoned for child abduction. *Child abduction! Wow.*

In prison, nothing and no-one is as they seem, after reading through B's paperwork, it became clear that she had been asked to sign a document effectively acknowledging she had received a court order which she hadn't.

I asked my Caseworker to help, as B's had made no contact and with limited English, she did not know what was going on.
There were many ladies here who made me question the justice system and how I could help them.

Ladies who felt prison was the only place they would be safe after trying to flee domestic violence following failed restraining orders, women playing the system so they would retain this place as a form of accommodation rather than return to a life of homelessness, fear and trauma. So much was going on here – *there is so much that needs to be done.*

I don't know why anyone would want to stay here, your sleep is repeatedly interrupted when officers come around to check on you. The first check just after 9pm is okay, but then a bright flashlight is shone through the hatch just after midnight, around 2am and again after 5am. If the officer is being horrid – like tonight, they can turn your cell lights on externally – you are then not able to switch them off! They bang on your door, flick the flashlight on and off and disturb your sleep. *Thank goodness I have not been sentenced to serve a long period of time.*

During my time I heard disturbing things, spoke with ladies, prayed with them, shared Psalms and other encouraging scripture verses, helped draft letters, read over case papers and ladies would often come to my cell to enquire whether I could assist them in some way. So to be approached was not unusual, but when this lady came into my cell the atmosphere changed.

I often use the phrase "It unsettles my spirit" – that is how I felt right now.
"You're the MP lady aren't you?" she asks as she enters my cell and closes the door. *I like my face! There is no way out – be diplomatic Fiona* I tell myself in the brief moment before I reply, "Yes I am, why?"

"Do you think I would get help if I write a letter? I mean, given their voting record, they don't believe this is a criminal offence right?."

I couldn't believe what I was hearing! This lady went on to advise she had been sentenced to several years. I recall hearing about this on the news. I ask some questions and she asks me whether I would like to see pictures. *Pictures?! OH MY GOODNESS, why on earth would she have pictures?* Why would she be allowed to keep pictures? "Absolutely not, I can't unsee things!" She sees the shock horror on my face and hears the distain in my voice. She stands over me – *I am praying silently in my head.*

Just as I'm trying to figure out how to respond diplomatically I hear the usual evening command "Ladies behind your doors" is being shouted.
Relief washes over me as she leaves the cell.

I was fortunate in that I never had any trouble and could articulate what was wrong. I was horrified that after Grenfell, in the event of a fire, we would remain locked in and our cell would be flooded out. I did not see a foam hose anywhere on the landing, just water and given that there was both a television and phone in the cell, the likelihood would be that any fire would be electrical – for which water could not be used!

There was never a fire, our cell was never spun and time had seemingly passed quite quickly.

It was early hours when the intercom came on in our cell –
"Miss Onasanya, can you get up and ready to leave please."
It's the day of my release.
I've been up since 5am! I've stripped the bed, folded the linen and am READY!

B is awake, I apologise for the squeal and loudness of my voice, "B I'm going home, I'm going home!" She smiles, we had discussed today between ourselves, having never previously offended I was deemed "Low risk".

I had been advised I should be in an open prison, but I would be kept here for costs sake, the letter from my Solicitors advised I should be eligible for Home Detention Curfew (HDC) due to the length of my sentence and as I was being released after 28 days, I would only be required to wear a tag for a further 2 weeks as I was sentenced to 3 months of which I was mandated to serve half (being 6 weeks).

It wasn't long until I heard the jingling of keys and steps coming up the landing. The footsteps stopped outside of our door, I hear the key turn in the lock and the officer invites me to leave.

I can't stop smiling, I ask the officer if he can help me with my bag and explain I have left all the prison items back in the white netted bag, stripped the bed and folded the linen. The officer escorts me out of the room. I ask if I can say goodbye, he opens the hatch and I wave goodbye to B, she smiles.

Walking over with the prison officer I explain I have learnt a lot and will endeavour to be a voice for these women outside.

As we speak I enquire why people are shouting? He explains that the shouting is coming from the health wing. I am saddened by this, "People with mental health issues are not criminals, they are unwell" he nods along as I add "You guys aren't mental health specialists, do you get given special training?" "Not really special per se" he replies, explaining that not only is mental heath complex, but the training (for some) is only adequate not specialist

We go through to the same reception I arrived at 28 days earlier. I speak to the officers who advise there are lots of press waiting for me! *How did they know I was here and that I was being released today?! I hadn't told anyone?!* We devised a plan to get me out and I thanked the officers. One of them asked me if I would return to speak to the ladies as they found me quite inspirational, "That's very kind, of course I'll come back – but not as an inmate!" With that I went to see the Dr, collected my things and walked to a white Sodexo branded vehicle. The driver had placed a high visibility jacket up in the window beside me to shield me from the press. He instructs security that all barriers need to be up as he wants to drive me straight out. He gets back into the car – I thank him, put the shades on and brace myself....Here we go!

We exit at speed and zoom past the waiting reporters.

The sodexo vehicle drops me at the pre-arranged location where I jump in with mum – she tells me I've lost weight and I ask if we can go to somewhere where *I can get a cup of ice!*

I put my seat back and sleep.

After some time we pull into my cul-de-sac "Oh no!" The press are gathered in their cars and numbers outside my home.

I can hear the snapping of cameras, *don't they have anyone else to bother, I just want a shower and my bed!*

I get out of the car and head to my door, closing the gate behind me without turning around. The press are calling my name as I put my key into the front door I turn the key, enter and close the door behind me. I'm home!!

There was a big vote in Parliament that week, but with the bombardment of the press including those swarming outside my home, I didn't go for that vote.

That following week (5 March 2019) I had to appear before the Court of Appeal, I was seeking permission to appeal the conviction – I didn't do what I had been convicted of so the conviction could not be correct.

Mum and I attended the Court of Appeal together.

I was confused, I'd read online that grounds go before a single Judge, if they are not correct your application for permission to appeal would be refused. However, I was advised, following my grounds being received, that I would be required to attend "Full court".

At court I did not have Counsel, I could not afford it. After 2 trials, all resources had been used – I even had to take out a loan! My legal costs were over £30k before we'd even got to the first trial and Counsel's costs had taken that figure to over £50k – I was not entitled to legal aid so had to find ways to finance the trial, and then it had to be done all over again!!

So here we were, the Judge commented on the fact I had no papers, *I didn't realise I had to bring anything, online it said you have to send everything in, which I had done?!* He asked if I wished to add anything further – I stood to make a brief submission and then the Judges retired.
It wasn't too long before the Judges returned.

It was explained that the Court of Appeal could only consider my case if; the Judge had made a mistake in directing the jury, there were errors in law or material irregularities. I felt I had set out the errors but apparently these were factual matters – which could not be considered by them. It seemed that although the police were wrong in asking the witnesses to 'Tighten up their timings', witness statements changing and other matters which I had put down as irregularities – were not matters which the Court could consider and as such my request for permission to appeal was refused.

I was asked by a member of the press if I wished to make a comment, despite my advising that I would not be making a comment, he joined with the other reporters and ran after me across the zebra crossing outside the Court!

It will be over soon.

The following week my tag was coming off! I could get back to working for my constituents.

Now it was different, my office staff had diminished, the abuse had increased, and my favourite door keepers had an element of concern in their tone – everyone's behaviour was egg-shellish.

I was even accused of "Perverting the course of Brexit" when I, along with 312 other MP's voted not to leave without a deal. I had always said we were leaving, the issue was not IF but rather HOW! It seemed I had become a target for the tabloids – but I never rose to it. To maintain a dignified silence was the best way to deal with foolish comments and behaviour, such as papers reporting I was on tag (when I was not!!).

The count down to the opening of the recall petition had begun, it was not too long after my release that I advised my staff I would not be standing in the by-election should the petition be successful – I was not prepared to splinter any vote – Labour needed to retain this seat.

Now my focus needed to be on clearing my name, restoring my character that the press sought to assassinate – now the journey truly begins.

Aside from this I also had the upcoming Employment Tribunal. One of my former employees was claiming I had discriminated against her on the grounds of disability.

CHAPTER 18

THE TRIBUNAL

This Tribunal had come about as the claimant had disagreed with the outcome of the independent HR advisor, as well as the outcome of the appeal against that decision. This Tribunal hearing was in addition to a number of other avenues sought by her – but thankfully it was the final leg of this saga.

It would now finally end.

I am here in Court (again!). Reporters are here and outside – although it doesn't feel as crazy as The Old Bailey trials.

The crux of this case was whether I, as an employer, had made reasonable adjustments to accommodate the employee. It seemed what was being asserted was that I had not done enough to cater for the "Iffy days", which were unbeknownst to me and essentially IF she could make it in.

I sat in silence as the claim was dismissed – but surprise surprise this was not widely reported.

However, this was not the end of this stormy journey in my life, no, this game of life, of Snakes and Adders was about to take another turn as months later, I was also struck off the Roll of Solicitors.

It now seemed to the outside world that I had lost it all – many believe this is the case.

CHAPTER 19

THE END?

This is not the end. Every ending is a new beginning, so I am excited to see what the next chapter holds as I turn the pages of life.

Just like flowers, I have heard it said that "We need dirt to grow" but actually, this journey has shown me, I am a seed. To be buried in dirt is the right environment for me to spring forth, I'm looking forward to seeing what is still to come.

Printed in Poland
by Amazon Fulfillment
Poland Sp. z o.o., Wrocław

54050799R00073